How to Use This Book

A Variety of Presentations

1. Make overhead transparencies of the lessons. Present each lesson as an oral activity with the entire class. Write answers and make corrections using an erasable marker.

   As the class becomes more familiar with *Daily Word Problems*, have students mark their answers first and then check them against correct responses marked on the transparency.

2. Reproduce the problems for individuals or partners to work on independently. Check answers as a group, using an overhead transparency to model the solutions' strategies. (Use these pages as independent practice only after much group experience with the lessons.)

3. Occasionally you may want to reproduce problems as a test to see how individuals are progressing in their acquisition of skills.

Important Considerations

1. Allow students to use whatever tools they need to solve problems. Some students will choose to use manipulatives, while others will want to make drawings. Calculators may be made available to allow students to focus on the solution process.

2. It is important that students share their solutions. Modeling a variety of problem-solving techniques makes students aware that there are different paths to the correct answer. Don't scrimp on the amount of time allowed for discussing how solutions were reached.

3. Teach students to follow problem-solving strategies:
   • Read the problem carefully more than one time. Think about it as you read.
   • Mark the important information in the problem.
   >   What question does the problem ask?
   >   What words will help you know how to solve the problem (*in all, left, how many more,* etc.)?
   >   What facts will help you answer the question? (Cross out facts that are NOT needed.)
   • Think about what you need to do to solve the problem (add, subtract, multiply, or divide).
   • Solve the problem. Does your answer make sense?
   • Check your answer.

Matrix Logic Puzzles

The Friday problems for weeks 5, 10, 13, 17, 22, 27, 34, and 36 are matrix logic puzzles. Here are some guidelines for helping students solve this type of logic puzzle:

   • Read all the clues. Find clues that give a definite *Yes* or *No*. (For example: John plays the clarinet. Sally does not play the flute.) Mark boxes with X (for no) or *Yes*.
   • When you mark a box *Yes*, mark Xs in all the other boxes in that row and in the column above and below the X.
   • Find clues that give information, but not enough to tell you how to mark the boxes. Make notes in the boxes for later use.
   • Go over each clue again. Look for clues that fit together to give enough information to make a box *Yes* or X (no).

Scope and Sequence—Grade 5

Week	1	2	3	4	5	6	7	8	9	10	11	12	13	14	15	16	17	18	19	20	21	22	23	24	25	26	27	28	29	30	31	32	33	34	35	36
Addition & Subtraction	•	•	•	•		•	•	•	•	•	•	•	•	•	•	•	•	•	•	•	•	•	•	•	•	•	•	•	•	•	•	•	•	•	•	•
1-Digit Multiplication	•	•		•		•	•	•	•	•	•	•	•	•	•	•	•	•	•	•	•	•	•	•	•	•	•	•	•	•	•	•	•	•	•	•
2- & 3-Digit Multiplication	•		•	•	•	•		•				•	•		•				•			•			•			•					•		•	
1-Digit Divisors				•	•	•	•				•		•			•		•	•	•			•			•		•			•	•	•	•	•	•
2- & 3-Digit Divisors			•			•	•							•			•	•		•			•				•	•		•		•	•	•	•	•
Fractions	•	•	•	•	•	•	•	•	•	•	•						•		•	•	•	•	•	•			•	•			•	•	•	•		
Decimals/Percents		•	•	•	•	•	•	•		•	•		•			•					•	•	•	•	•	•			•					•		
Time	•					•		•		•		•			•	•	•	•				•	•	•		•	•			•	•	•	•	•		
Money	•			•	•	•					•			•				•	•	•	•				•		•	•		•		•	•	•	•	•
Linear Measurement					•	•					•			•						•	•	•			•		•									•
Weight and Capacity									•				•				•			•				•	•				•					•		
Interpreting Graphs		•		•		•						•	•			•		•	•		•					•						•				
Geometry			•		•				•						•							•													•	
Data/Probability			•					•					•				•					•	•		•			•	•	•	•				•	
Logic	•				•				•	•							•			•	•	•	•	•		•								•		
Averages, Mode, Range	•	•	•				•			•				•			•	•														•			•	
Area/Perimeter			•								•				•					•				•	•		•		•			•	•		•	•

©2001 by Evan-Moor Corp.

2

Daily Word Problems
Monday-Week 1

School Carnival

Polk Elementary School was putting on its annual fall carnival. The school was selling 10 tickets for $1.00 or 2 tickets for 25¢. Which is the better buy? Explain why.

Name:

Work Space:

Answer:

_____

_____

_____

_____

Daily Word Problems
Tuesday-Week 1

School Carnival

The line for the Dunking Machine was twice as long as the Cake Walk line. The line for the Cake Walk was one-third the length of the line for the Hoop Shoot. If there were 12 people in line for the Hoop Shoot, how many people were in line for the Dunking Machine?

Name:

Work Space:

Answer:

_____ people

Daily Word Problems
Wednesday–Week 1

School Carnival

Polk Elementary School has three classes for each grade level, kindergarten through fifth grade. If there is an average of 27 students per classroom, about how many students attend Polk Elementary School?

Name:

Work Space:

Answer:

_____ students

Daily Word Problems
Thursday–Week 1

School Carnival

The school made $2,800 on the school carnival. The second- and fifth-grade classes each made only $200. The kindergarten and fourth-grade classes each made double the second grade's amount. The first and third grades made the same amount of money. How much did each grade level make?

Name:

Work Space:

Answer:

Kindergarten $_____

1st Grade $_____

2nd Grade $_____

3rd Grade $_____

4th Grade $_____

5th Grade $_____

Daily Word Problems

Name:

School Carnival

Many of the students went to the Beanbag Toss game at the school carnival. Each student got to throw beanbags until five beanbags went through the holes.

The following scores were reported for five students:

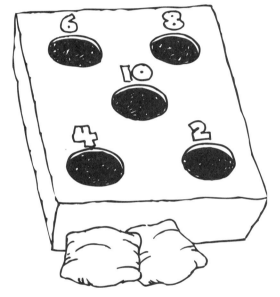

　　Timmy says he got 40 points.

　　Penny says she got 56 points.

　　Judy says she got 36 points.

　　Ian says he got 45 points.

　　Amber says she got 42 points.

Two of the students made errors in adding up their scores. Which students made errors? Explain your answer.

_____

_____

_____

_____

 Daily Word Problems • EMC 3005

Daily Word Problems

Chocolate Factory

Monday-Week 2

The Melt in Your Mouth Chocolate Factory is a rectangular building. The distance across the front of the store is 294 feet. The distance from the front to the back is one-third of this distance. If the owners paint a sign all the way around the outside of the factory, how many feet long will the sign be?

Name:

Work Space:

Answer:

_____ feet

Daily Word Problems

Chocolate Factory

Tuesday-Week 2

The Melt in Your Mouth Chocolate Factory sells three times as many Mints as it sells Almond Bars. It sells half as many Almond Bars as it sells Caramels. If it sells 3,750 cases of Mints each month, how many Caramels does it sell in one month?

Name:

Work Space:

Answer:

_____ Caramels

Daily Word Problems

Wednesday-Week 2

Chocolate Factory

Each case of Almond Bars contains 9 smaller boxes. Each smaller box contains 24 Almond Bars. How many Almond Bars are in each case?

Name:

Work Space:

Answer:

_____ Almond Bars

Daily Word Problems

Thursday-Week 2

Chocolate Factory

The Melt in Your Mouth Chocolate Factory opens its doors each day at 7:00 a.m. sharp. Sally arrived at the factory 10 minutes before the doors opened. Luke got there 18 minutes after Sally, but 4 minutes before Michelle. At what time did Michelle arrive at the factory?

Name:

Work Space:

Answer:

_____

Daily Word Problems

Name:

Chocolate Factory

The following graph shows the candy sales for the last year.

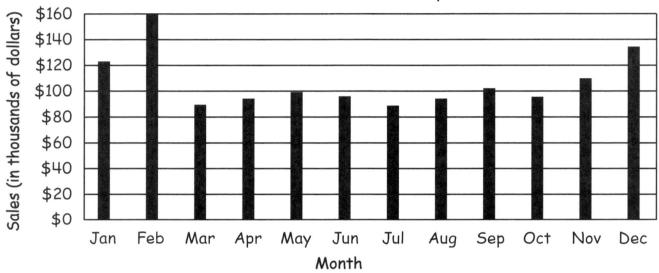

Melt in Your Mouth Candy Sales

• What are the two highest months of sales?

_____

• What are some possible explanations for the increase in sales during those two months?

_____

_____

_____

• How much more was sold in February than in May?

_____

Daily Word Problems

Monday-Week 3

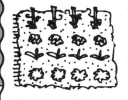

Garden Harvest

Mr. Garcia's class is harvesting the school garden. The rectangular garden is twenty-five feet by fifteen feet. What is the area of the garden?

Name:

Work Space:

Answer:

_____ square feet

Daily Word Problems

Tuesday-Week 3

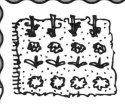

Garden Harvest

Felipe picked a pumpkin that weighed three times the weight of Meg's pumpkin. Meg's pumpkin was half the weight of Ryan's pumpkin. Ryan's pumpkin weighed 14 pounds. How much did Felipe's pumpkin weigh?

Name:

Work Space:

Answer:

_____ pounds

Daily Word Problems

Wednesday-Week 3

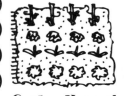

Garden Harvest

Kathy and George are in charge of picking the cherry tomatoes. They picked a huge bushel of 744 tomatoes. They want to pack them in little baskets that can each hold 24 tomatoes. How many baskets will they need to pack the tomatoes?

Name:

Work Space:

Answer:

_____ baskets

Daily Word Problems

Thursday-Week 3

Garden Harvest

Five different varieties of flowers are growing in the garden: carnations, roses, mums, marigolds, and lilies. Peter and Juanita are responsible for picking flowers and arranging them in vases to sell. They use three different types of flowers in each vase. For example, one vase might contain roses, carnations, and lilies. How many different combinations can be made from the five varieties of flowers?

Name:

Work Space:

Answer:

_____ combinations

Name:

Garden Harvest

The following table shows the vegetables that six students picked.

Name of Student	Produce Picked	Number of Items Picked	Total Weight of Items Picked
John	cucumbers	92	25 pounds
Veronica	tomatoes	84	19 pounds
Ted	watermelons	15	45 pounds
Melissa	peppers	75	15 pounds
Susan	corn	73	25 pounds
Timothy	squash	32	9 pounds

• According to the table, how many items in all were picked from the garden?

_____

• What was the average weight of the watermelons?

_____

• What was the average weight of the peppers?

_____

Daily Word Problems

Monday-Week 4

Arcade Games

John's high score on the Asteroid Game was 326,700. Mike's high score was 418,200. Rebecca just played the game and her high score was halfway between John's and Mike's. What was Rebecca's score?

Name:

Work Space:

Answer:

_____ points

Daily Word Problems

Tuesday-Week 4

Arcade Games

The arcade has three pinball machines and five video games. If a person wants to play one pinball machine and one video game, how many different combinations of games could that person play?

Name:

Work Space:

Answer:

_____ combinations

Daily Word Problems

Wednesday–Week 4

Arcade Games

The game Raceway allows you to earn 125 points for each car you pass during the race. When James played Raceway, he passed 27 cars. How many points did he earn for passing the cars?

Name:

Work Space:

Answer:

_____ points

Daily Word Problems

Thursday–Week 4

Arcade Games

David, Jenny, and Dan went to the arcade on Wednesday. David spent $3.25. Jenny spent $2.25 more than Dan, who spent $1.75 less than David. How much did they spend in all?

Name:

Work Space:

Answer:

$_____

Daily Word Problems

Friday-Week 4

Arcade Games

On the following map, the gray box shows the location of the arcade. Each letter represents a different student's house.

North ↑

									L			
A							H					R
		D									P	
					F	I	J					S
		C						M		Q		
					G							
	B						K		O			
				E								T

Nikki followed the directions below and ended up at the arcade.

Go five blocks north.
Go three blocks west.
Go four blocks south to your friend's house.
Go six blocks east.
Go two blocks north to the arcade.

• At what letter house did she start from? _____

• What letter was her friend's house? _____

Daily Word Problems

Monday—Week 5

Camping Trip

During the fifth-grade camping trip, nine students can sleep in each cabin. All boys or all girls must sleep in each cabin. If there are 70 boys and 76 girls in the fifth grade, how many cabins will be needed to house all of the students?

Name:

Work Space:

Answer:

_____ cabins

Daily Word Problems

Tuesday—Week 5

Camping Trip

The camping trip costs $25.00 per student. If there are 146 students going on the trip, how much money will the fifth-grade class need in all?

Name:

Work Space:

Answer:

$_____

Daily Word Problems

Wednesday-Week 5

Camping Trip

Jim's sleeping bag is 5 feet long. Jorge's sleeping bag is 2 yards long. Steven's sleeping bag is 68 inches long. Whose sleeping bag is the longest?

Name:

Work Space:

Answer:

_____

Daily Word Problems

Thursday-Week 5

Camping Trip

The boys' cabins are all shaped with a rectangular prism on the bottom and a triangular prism on the top. The girls' cabins are all shaped with a rectangular prism on the bottom and a rectangular pyramid on the top. Draw the shape of each cabin.

Name:

Answer:

Daily Word Problems

Friday-Week 5

Camping Trip

Use the clues below to determine the first and last names of the six boys who were in one of the cabins.

When you know that a first and last name do **not** go with each other, make an **X** under the last name and across from the first name. When you know that a first and last name do go together, write **YES** in that box. You can then **X** that first name and last name for all others.

	Bucklen	Mitchell	Sari	McClain	Moore	Brown
George						
Mike						
Raul						
Sam						
Saul						
Tim						

Clues:

1. Neither Mike nor Raul has the last name of Moore or Brown.

2. George and the Bucklen boy live next door to each other.

3. Saul Mitchell and Tim Sari compete in the local dance competitions.

4. The Bucklen boy and Sam are best friends.

5. Raul's initials are R.M.

6. Each boy has different initials.

Daily Word Problems

Monday-Week 6

Dog Walking

Marcy decided to start a new business of walking dogs. She designed a flier to advertise her business to her neighbors. She had 100 fliers printed. The copy center charged 7¢ per copy for the first ten copies and then 5¢ for each additional copy. What was the total cost of the fliers?

Name:

Work Space:

Answer:

$ _____

Daily Word Problems

Tuesday-Week 6

Dog Walking

After school, Marcy can start walking dogs by 3:15 p.m. She wants to be done walking the dogs by 6:00 p.m. so she can get home in time for dinner. If she schedules each dog walk for a half hour and then allows herself fifteen minutes between each walk to get to the next house, how many dogs can she walk before dinnertime?

Name:

Work Space:

Answer:

_____ dogs

Daily Word Problems
Wednesday-Week 6

Dog Walking

Marcy charges $3 to walk a small dog and $5 to walk a big dog. If Marcy walks 15 small dogs and 6 big dogs, how much money will she make?

Name:

Work Space:

Answer:

$ _____

Daily Word Problems
Thursday-Week 6

Dog Walking

Marcy can walk 12 blocks in 5 minutes. If each block is about 50 feet long, how many feet will she walk during the 30 minutes that she walks each dog?

Name:

Work Space:

Answer:

_____ feet

Daily Word Problems

Name:

Dog Walking

The following graph shows the dogs that Marcy walks.

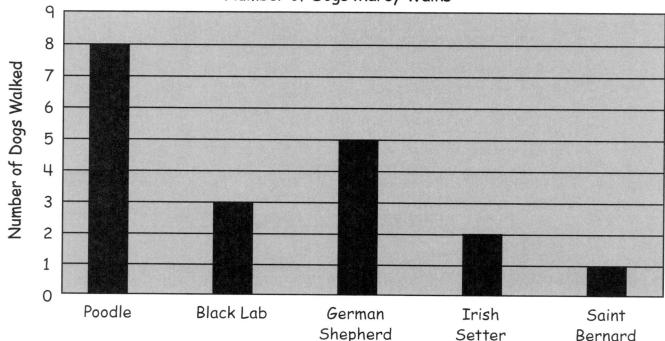

Number of Dogs Marcy Walks

Number of Dogs Walked

Poodle   Black Lab   German Shepherd   Irish Setter   Saint Bernard

Types of Dogs

• How many dogs in all does Marcy walk?

_____

• Some of the bars equal the sum of two smaller bars. How many sets of three bars fall in this category where the sum of the two smaller bars equals the one larger bar? Show your work.

_____

_____

_____

Daily Word Problems

Monday-Week 7

Reading

Jimmy read half the amount of time that Heather read. Heather read only one-fourth the time that Connor read. Connor read twice as long as Laura. If Laura read for 2 hours, how long did Jimmy read?

Name:

Work Space:

Answer:

_____

Daily Word Problems

Tuesday-Week 7

Reading

Juan read 14 books during the month. Samantha read 26 books during the month. Lori read 18 books during the month. Scott read 22 books during the month. What was the average number of books read by these four students during the month?

Name:

Work Space:

Answer:

_____ books

Daily Word Problems

Wednesday-Week 7

Reading

Six books stand on the bookshelf. The widths of the books are 1.2 cm, 0.8 cm, 2.4 cm, 1.9 cm, 1.5 cm, and 2.3 cm. What is the total width of the six books on the bookshelf?

Name:

Work Space:

Answer:

_____ cm

Daily Word Problems

Thursday-Week 7

Reading

Ms. Watson's class read for a total of 450 hours this month. Mr. Gerk's class read two-thirds the number of hours read by Ms. Watson's class. Miss Rupp's class read twice the number of hours read by Mr. Gerk's class. If there were a total of 90 students in these three classrooms, what was the average number of hours read per student?

Name:

Work Space:

Answer:

_____ hours per student

Daily Word Problems

Name:

Reading

Use the following three graphs to answer the
questions below.

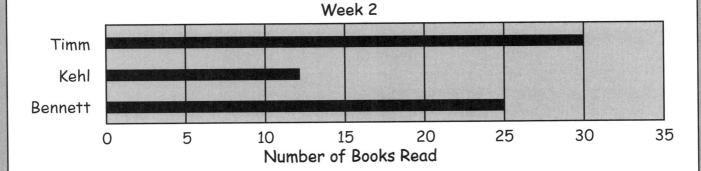

Week 1

Timm
Kehl
Bennett

0 5 10 15 20 25 30 35 40
Number of Books Read

Week 2

Timm
Kehl
Bennett

0 5 10 15 20 25 30 35
Number of Books Read

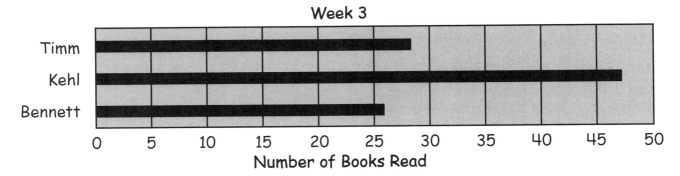

Week 3

Timm
Kehl
Bennett

0 5 10 15 20 25 30 35 40 45 50
Number of Books Read

• Which class read the most books during the three-week reading event?

_____

• For each classroom, what was the average number of books read per week
during the three weeks?

_____ _____ _____

Daily Word Problems

Monday–Week 8

Music Lessons

Jim's piano lessons are 30 minutes longer than Suzanne's clarinet lessons. Suzanne's clarinet lessons are one-third the length of Pedro's guitar lessons. If Pedro's guitar lessons are 60 minutes long, how long are Jim and Suzanne's lessons?

Name:

Work Space:

Answer:

Jim's _____

Suzanne's _____

Daily Word Problems

Tuesday–Week 8

Music Lessons

The City Piano Association is giving a mass piano concert. They brought in 24 pianos and had them all on one stage. The piano tuner is coming to tune the pianos. If each piano has 88 keys, how many keys in all will the piano tuner have to tune?

Name:

Work Space:

Answer:

_____ keys

Daily Word Problems

Wednesday-Week 8

Music Lessons

The perimeter of the rectangular-shaped base of a piano is 16 feet. What are all the possible dimensions of the piano, using only whole numbers of feet?

Name:

Work Space:

Answer:

_____

_____

Daily Word Problems

Thursday-Week 8

Music Lessons

The names, or notes, of all the white keys on a piano are written on pieces of paper and placed in a cup. There are 7 sets of the notes D, E, F, and G and 8 sets of the notes A, B, and C. If a person draws one note out of the cup without looking, what are his or her chances of getting a C?

Name:

Work Space:

Answer:

_____

Daily Word Problems

Friday-Week 8

Name:

Music Lessons

Ralph is going to the music store to buy some new strings for his guitar. He needs to replace 6 of the 12 strings on his guitar.

INDIVIDUAL GUITAR STRINGS

Deluxe

First four strings are $6.25 each

Additional strings are $4.75 each

Regular

First four strings are $5.00 each

Additional strings are $3.75 each

- How much will he save if he buys the regular strings instead of the deluxe strings?

_____

Daily Word Problems
Monday-Week 9

Pets

Holly has 25 fish in her aquarium. Tommy has one-fifth the number of fish that Holly has. Jared has three times as many fish as Tommy. If they were to combine all their fish in the new school aquarium, how many fish would there be in all?

Name:

Work Space:

Answer:

_____ fish

Daily Word Problems
Tuesday-Week 9

Pets

Beth has hamsters at her house. The number of hamsters is equal to the sum of the number of birds at Kristin's house and the number of dogs at Wendi's house. John has the same number of cats as Wendi has of dogs. If these four children have a total of 12 pets, how many pets are at each house?

Name:

Work Space:

Answer:

_____ hamsters at Beth's house

_____ birds at Kristin's house

_____ dogs at Wendi's house

_____ cats at John's house

Daily Word Problems

Wednesday-Week 9

Pets

Tyler has two dogs. One of the dogs weighs twice as much as the other. If the total weight of the two dogs is 60 pounds, how much does each dog weigh?

Name:

Work Space:

Answer:

_____

Daily Word Problems

Thursday-Week 9

Pets

Juan is constructing a doghouse. He needs four pieces of plywood that are 2 ft x 3 ft rectangles. He needs two pieces of plywood that are 2 ft x 2 ft squares. If the plywood comes in 4 ft x 8 ft sheets, what is the minimum number of sheets of plywood Juan will need?

Name:

Work Space:

Answer:

_____

Name: _____

Pets

The following shape is a floor plan for a dog run that is in Jorge's backyard. Use the clues below to determine the dimensions of each side of the dog run.

F _____

_____ A

B _____

_____ C

E _____

D _____

Clues:

1. The total perimeter of the dog run is 36 feet.

2. The length of E is equal to the sum of A and C.

3. The length of F is equal to the sum of B and D.

4. The length of E is 8 feet.

5. A, B, C, and D are consecutive numbers, in that order.

Daily Word Problems

Monday-Week 10

Car Racing

Jimmy, Joe, and Sally are racing their cars. Jimmy and Joe have completed the same number of laps—six fewer laps than Sally. If the total number of completed laps is 222, how many laps has each of the three racers completed?

Name:

Work Space:

Answer:

_____
_____
_____

Daily Word Problems

Tuesday-Week 10

Car Racing

Ruth's car traveled 120 miles during the first race. During the second race, it traveled 124 miles. If the car averaged 123 miles over the first three races, how far did it travel during the third race?

Name:

Work Space:

Answer:

_____ miles

Daily Word Problems
Wednesday-Week 10

Car Racing

Juan's pit crew was able to get his car back onto the racetrack 0.8 second faster than Paul's crew. Paul's crew took 1.2 seconds longer than Terry's crew. Terry's crew took 5.2 seconds to complete their pit stop. How long did Juan's crew take?

Name:

Work Space:

Answer:

_____ seconds

Daily Word Problems
Thursday-Week 10

Car Racing

During the last five races, Jim's race car used an average of 15 gallons of gas per race. If his race car used a total of 51 gallons of gas during the first three races, what was the total number of gallons of gas used during the last two races?

Name:

Work Space:

Answer:

_____ gallons

Daily Word Problems

Car Racing

Use the clues below to determine the first and last name of each race car driver.

When you know that a first and last name do **not** go with each other, make an **X** under the last name and across from the first name. When you know that a first and last name do go together, write **YES** in that box. You can then **X** that first name and last name for all others.

	Brown	Chavez	Jones	Tjardes	Turnwall
Angel					
Austin					
Ben					
George					
Sarah					

Clues:

1. No one's first name starts with the same first letter as his/her last name.

2. Two of the drivers have the same initials.

3. Sarah Chavez wins the race.

4. Turnwall finished two places after Austin.

Daily Word Problems

Monday-Week 11

Shopping Mall

In the local mall there are twice as many clothing stores as there are music stores. There are twice as many music stores as there are computer stores. If there are 16 clothing stores, how many computer stores are in the mall?

Name:

Work Space:

Answer:

_____ computer stores

Daily Word Problems

Tuesday-Week 11

Shopping Mall

Music World is having a huge sale. They are selling every item at half price. Sam wants to buy three CDs that were originally priced at $7.98, $14.00, and $12.96. What will be Sam's total?

Name:

Work Space:

Answer:

$_____

Daily Word Problems

Wednesday-Week 11

Shopping Mall

Julie is going to the mall. She has 15 coins in her pocket that add up to $2.18. She has the same number of pennies as she does dimes. She has 5 more quarters than she has nickels. If she has 3 pennies, how many quarters, dimes, and nickels does Julie have?

Name:

Work Space:

Answer:

_____ quarters

_____ dimes

_____ nickels

Daily Word Problems

Thursday-Week 11

Shopping Mall

Dan was walking from one end of the mall to the other end. He took the following measurements of five storefronts: 23 feet 11 inches, 25 feet 2 inches, 18 feet 3 inches, 28 feet 8 inches, and 32 feet 4 inches. If Dan added all the measurements, what would be the total distance?

Name:

Work Space:

Answer:

_____

Name:

The following figures represent the floor plans for two different stores. Circle the store that gives the largest amount of area to put out display racks and shelves for customers.

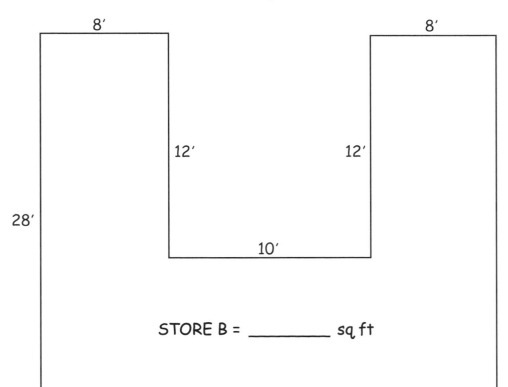

12′

5′

16′

STORE A = _____ sq ft

12′

28′

8′   8′

12′   12′

28′

10′

STORE B = _____ sq ft

Daily Word Problems

Monday-Week 12

Homework

Mrs. Johnson gives twice as much daily homework as Mr. Beach. Mr. Beach gives 10 minutes less than Mrs. Rodriguez. If Mrs. Rodriguez gives 35 minutes of homework, what is the total amount of homework given by the three teachers?

Name:

Work Space:

Answer:

_____ minutes of homework

Daily Word Problems

Tuesday-Week 12

Homework

Samantha has homework in five subjects tonight. She has 15 minutes of science, 20 minutes of math, 30 minutes of reading, 20 minutes of writing, and 15 minutes of geography. If her mom walked in randomly while she was doing her homework, what subject would she most likely see Samantha working on?

Name:

Work Space:

Answer:

_____

Daily Word Problems

Wednesday-Week 12

Homework

George is averaging 45 minutes of homework each school night. Most of the time, George has school five days a week, and his school year lasts for 36 weeks. About how many minutes of homework will he do throughout the entire school year?

Name:

Work Space:

Answer:

_____ minutes

Daily Word Problems

Thursday-Week 12

Homework

During the week, five students kept track of how much time they spent doing homework. Jonathan did 185 minutes, Susan did 205 minutes, Doug did 240 minutes, Sharon did 95 minutes, and Bo did 155 minutes. What was the total number of minutes the students spent on their homework? What is the difference between the most and the least amount of homework time?

Name:

Work Space:

Answer:

_____ minutes

_____ minutes' difference

Daily Word Problems
Friday-Week 12

Homework

The circle graph represents a total of 200 minutes of homework that Marla did during the week.

Number of Minutes of Homework in Each Subject

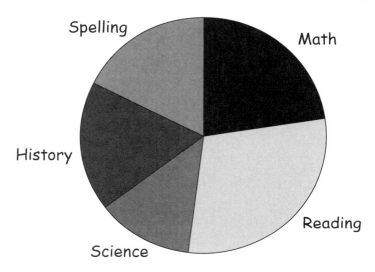

Estimate the number of minutes Marla spent doing homework in each subject area.

_____

_____

_____

_____

_____

Daily Word Problems

Monday–Week 13

Recycling

As a project, the fifth-grade students at Scott Elementary School collected newspapers to recycle. During the first week, they collected 212 pounds of newspapers. For each of the next four weeks, they doubled the previous week's amount of newspapers collected. What was the total number of pounds of newspapers collected during the five weeks?

Name:

Work Space:

Answer:

_____ pounds

Daily Word Problems

Tuesday–Week 13

Recycling

Tim's family was collecting aluminum cans to recycle. They found out that they would get two cents for every three cans they collected. If they collected 2,187 cans, how much money did they receive?

Name:

Work Space:

Answer:

$_____

Daily Word Problems

Wednesday-Week 13

Recycling

Bettler Elementary School was recycling their copier paper after the students had completed the worksheets. They found that when they filled a barrel with paper, it weighed an average of 463 pounds. If they collected 16 barrels of paper during the year, what was the approximate weight of the paper?

Name:

Work Space:

Answer:

_____ pounds

Daily Word Problems

Thursday-Week 13

Recycling

John Brown Elementary School Art Club was recycling paper towel tubes for their holiday crafts project. The school's enrollment was 629 students. If the Art Club asked every student to bring 6 empty paper towel tubes to make the project, how many paper towel tubes did they need?

Name:

Work Space:

Answer:

_____ tubes

Daily Word Problems

Friday-Week 13

Recycling

Use the clues below to figure out how many pounds of cans each classroom brought in during their first week of recycling.

When you know that a room and number of pounds do **not** go with each other, make an **X** under the pounds and across from the room. When you know that a room and number of pounds do go together, write **YES** in that box. You can then **X** that room and number of pounds for all others.

	7 lbs	10 lbs	12 lbs	15 lbs	18 lbs	23 lbs
Room 2						
Room 4						
Room 6						
Room 7						
Room 9						
Room 10						

Clues:

1. None of the room numbers is the same as the number of pounds of cans collected by that room.

2. The sum of the weight of cans collected by Rooms 4 and 9 equals 30 pounds.

3. The weight of cans collected by Room 7 was 8 more than Room 10.

4. Room 9 collected 2 more pounds of cans than Room 2.

5. Room 6 collected the most cans.

Daily Word Problems

Monday-Week 14

Laundry

The Johnson family has been very busy and has not done their laundry for several weeks. The dirty laundry pile consists of 540 items of clothing. They figure they can put an average of 27 pieces of clothing in a single load. How many loads of laundry will the Johnson family have to do to wash all the items of clothing?

Name:

Work Space:

Answer:

_____ loads

Daily Word Problems

Tuesday-Week 14

Laundry

Ruth's brother just went away to college this fall and had to buy his own laundry soap and fabric softener. The laundry soap was twice the cost of the fabric softener. The total of the two items was $7.47. How much did the laundry soap and the fabric softener cost individually?

Name:

Work Space:

Answer:

laundry soap $_____

fabric softener $_____

Daily Word Problems

Wednesday-Week 14

Laundry

At Soap and Suds there are 16 washing machines in a single row with no space between each one. Each washing machine is 2 feet 5 inches across. What is the total length of the 16 washing machines?

Name:

Work Space:

Answer:

_____

Daily Word Problems

Thursday-Week 14

Laundry

In the dryer there are 18 red socks, 24 white socks, 8 blue socks, and 10 black socks. Fred wants to have two matching socks to wear. He reaches into the dryer and without looking pulls out one sock at a time. What is the minimum number of socks he needs to pull out to be sure he will have a matching pair? Why?

Name:

Work Space:

Answer:

_____

_____

_____

_____

Name:

Laundry

The following chart shows the number of minutes that a washing machine took to wash five different loads of laundry.

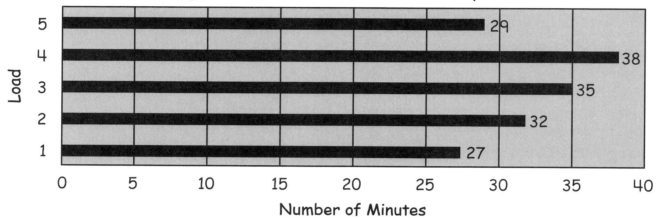

Length of Time to Wash Loads of Laundry

Load: 5 — 29, 4 — 38, 3 — 35, 2 — 32, 1 — 27

Number of Minutes

• What was the average length of time for the five loads?

_____

Daily Word Problems

Monday-Week 15

City Bus

Victor's class is going on a field trip. They will ride on the city bus twice, once going and once coming back. The one-way bus trip costs 35¢ per child and 50¢ per adult. There are 24 students, 4 parents, and 1 teacher going on the trip. How much money will they need for everyone to ride the bus?

Name:

Work Space:

Answer:

$_____

Daily Word Problems

Tuesday-Week 15

City Bus

Mrs. Kula's class was going on a bus trip. They left the school at 9:30 a.m. The bus trip to the zoo took 1 hour 15 minutes. They stayed at the zoo for 3 hours and then went to the park for 50 minutes before boarding the buses to return to school. At what time did they board the buses?

Name:

Work Space:

Answer:

_____

Daily Word Problems

Wednesday-Week 15

City Bus

The city bus is 45 feet long and 10 feet wide. The maintenance crew wants to paint two yellow stripes around the outside of the bus. What will be the total length of the two yellow stripes?

Name:

Work Space:

Answer:

_____ feet

Daily Word Problems

Thursday-Week 15

City Bus

The city has a fleet of 27 buses. Each bus can seat 44 people at a time. If all the buses were in use at the same time and each bus was full, how many people would be seated on all 27 buses?

Name:

Work Space:

Answer:

_____ people

Daily Word Problems

Name:

City Bus

The picture below is the logo for the city bus system.

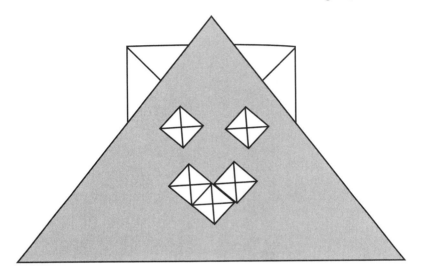

• How many triangles do you see in the figure? _____

Daily Word Problems

Monday-Week 16

Hot-Air Balloons

There is a hot-air balloon festival in System Springs. Seventy-two balloons registered to participate, paying $25 each. Five of those registered didn't show up and were refunded half of their money. Three additional balloons showed up and paid the registration cost plus an additional $10 each. What was the total amount of money collected after the five partial refunds were paid?

Name:

Work Space:

Answer:

$_____

Daily Word Problems

Tuesday-Week 16

Hot-Air Balloons

At a balloon festival, 268 people showed up to watch the evening lift-off on Friday night at 8:00 p.m. Saturday morning's lift-off brought in 328 people. Sunday morning's show brought in twice as many people as Friday night's lift-off. How many people in all came to watch the balloon festival?

Name:

Work Space:

Answer:

_____ people

Daily Word Problems
Wednesday-Week 16

Hot-Air Balloons

As several teams of hot-air balloons were setting up, the temperature was only 38.5 degrees. They had to wait for the temperature to go up. The temperature went up 7.2 degrees the first hour. During the second hour, the temperature rose another 13 degrees. By 11 o'clock the temperature had risen another 2.6 degrees. What was the temperature at 11 o'clock?

Name:

Work Space:

Answer:

_____ degrees

Daily Word Problems
Thursday-Week 16

Hot-Air Balloons

The fifth-grade classes at Martinez Elementary School are going to take a short tethered ride in a hot-air balloon. The balloon can hold three students at a time. If there are one hundred twenty-six students in the fifth grade, how many rides will have to be taken in order for every student to have a turn?

Name:

Work Space:

Answer:

_____ rides

Daily Word Problems

Name:

Hot-Air Balloons

The following graph shows the number of adults and children who watched the balloons lift off each week for seven weeks.

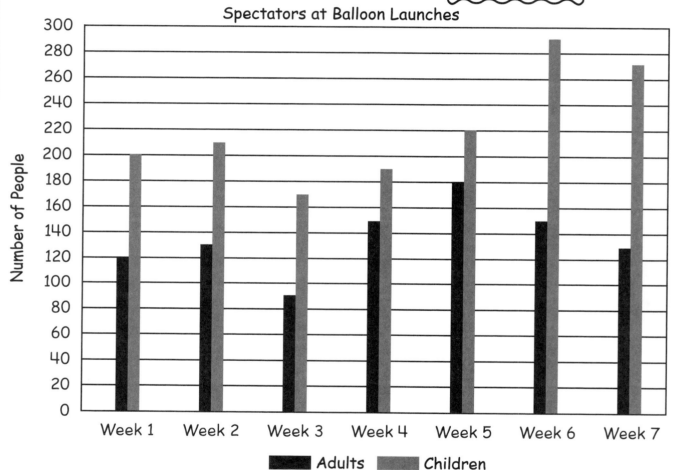

- What is the range of the data for the adults? _____

- What is the total number of children who attended the seven weeks of balloon lift-offs? _____

Daily Word Problems

Monday-Week 17

Travel

Sidney flew in an airplane five times during her vacation. The flights averaged 2 hours 28 minutes long. The lengths of her first four flights were 2 hours 10 minutes, 3 hours 20 minutes, 1 hour 15 minutes, and 2 hours 40 minutes. What was the length of her last flight?

Name:

Work Space:

Answer:

_____

Daily Word Problems

Tuesday-Week 17

Travel

Russell was scheduled to leave on his vacation when a major snowstorm came through and canceled three-fourths of the flights out of the airport. There were 496 flights scheduled for that day. How many flights were able to leave the airport?

Name:

Work Space:

Answer:

_____ flights

Daily Word Problems

Wednesday-Week 17

Travel

Four people in Abe's family are traveling to Canada for their vacation. They have four seats in the center section of the plane. Abe wants to sit next to his brother Ben. In how many different ways can the 4 people be seated so that Abe and Ben can sit next to each other? One way has been done for you.

Abe   Ben   Mom   Dad

Name:

Work Space:

Answer:

_____ ways

Daily Word Problems

Thursday-Week 17

Travel

The sign in the hotel elevator reads "Maximum of 6 people or 1200 lbs." Suzanne weighs 80 pounds, her dad is three times her weight, and her mom is twice her weight. Her sister is 40 pounds heavier than Suzanne, while her brother is 90 pounds heavier. Can they all ride in the elevator at the same time? Explain your answer.

Name:

Work Space:

Answer:

_____

_____

_____

_____

Daily Word Problems

Friday-Week 17

Travel

Use the clues below to determine the flight number for each family's flight.

When you know that a family and a flight number do **not** go with each other, make an **X** under the flight number and across from the family. When you know that a family and a flight number do go together, write **YES** in that box. You can then X that family and flight number for all others.

	1428	1536	1726	1834	2608
Stang					
Fortner					
Christopher					
Fitch					
Smythe					

Clues:

1. The sum of the flight numbers for the Stang and Fortner families was 3,262.

2. The Christopher family's flight number was bigger than the Fitch family's flight number.

3. The Stang family's flight number was either 1726 or 2608.

4. The Fortner family's flight number was 108 more than the Smythe family's flight number.

Daily Word Problems

Monday-Week 18

Family Reunion

Hector's extended family was gathering for a family reunion. There were 8 sets of aunts and uncles. There were twice as many cousins as uncles. There were two grandparents, and then there was Hector's family of five. How many people were at the reunion?

Name:

Work Space:

Answer:

_____ people

Daily Word Problems

Tuesday-Week 18

Family Reunion

Kayleen's family was traveling to the family reunion by car. They traveled 520 miles the first day and 380 miles the second day. If they averaged 60 miles an hour, how many hours were they on the road?

Name:

Work Space:

Answer:

_____ hours

Daily Word Problems

Wednesday-Week 18

Family Reunion

Tony's family wants to arrive at the family reunion at 5:00 p.m. for the supper that is being planned. Driving time will be about 6 hours 30 minutes. They plan to stop for gas one time for approximately 10 minutes. They also plan to stop for lunch for about 45 minutes. At what time should they leave in order to arrive by 5:00 p.m.?

Name:

Work Space:

Answer:

_____

Daily Word Problems

Thursday-Week 18

Family Reunion

There are 37 people attending the Ruiz family reunion, and they want to split the cost of the present for the grandparents. If the gift costs $464.72, how much should each person contribute?

Name:

Work Space:

Answer:

$_____

Name:

Family Reunion

Use the bar graph to answer the questions about the ages of the people at the family reunion.

Ages of People at Reunion

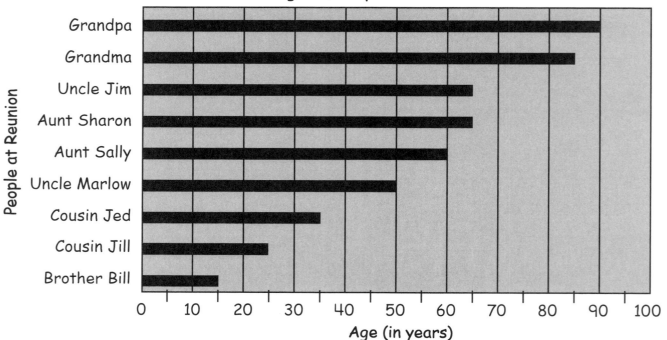

People at Reunion: Grandpa, Grandma, Uncle Jim, Aunt Sharon, Aunt Sally, Uncle Marlow, Cousin Jed, Cousin Jill, Brother Bill

Age (in years)

- What is the range of the ages of the nine people? _____

- What is the median age of those people? _____

Daily Word Problems

Monday-Week 19

Television Commercials

Seven companies each agreed to pay $120,000 for commercial spots at the local television station. What was the total paid to the television station by all seven companies?

Name:

Work Space:

Answer:

$_____

Daily Word Problems

Tuesday-Week 19

Television Commercials

One of the TV commercials uses a logo that is constructed from a black cube and two white square pyramids attached on opposite faces of the cube. The pyramids have a base equal in size to a face of the black cube. Draw what the figure looks like.

Name:

Answer:

Daily Word Problems

Wednesday-Week 19

Television Commercials

Hanson's Company is purchasing $45,000 worth of commercials. They agreed to pay for it in 6 equal payments over the next 6 months. How much will each monthly payment be in order to pay the entire amount by the end of the 6 months?

Name:

Work Space:

Answer:

$_____

Daily Word Problems

Thursday-Week 19

Television Commercials

Hudson Company is taping commercials for several companies. They need 20 minutes of commercials. They have already taped twenty-six 15-second commercials, fifteen 30-second commercials, and four 1-minute commercials. How much time do they have left?

Name:

Work Space:

Answer:

_____

Name:

Television Commercials

King Shoppers wants to create a commercial. They want to have a finished commercial that is 30 seconds in length. Use the following price chart to determine their costs.

Initial Set-up Costs $2,000

The additional charge depends on the length of the taping. Each taping will fall into one of the following price ranges:

1–5	Seconds of Finished Tape	$200/second
6–15	Seconds of Finished Tape	$150/second
16–30	Seconds of Finished Tape	$125/second
31–60	Seconds of Finished Tape	$110/second

Daily Word Problems

Monday-Week 20

Fire Stations

Galeton has three times the number of fire stations as Pierce, which has half as many fire stations as Evans. Evans has three more fire stations than Longmont. If Longmont has 5 fire stations, how many fire stations does Galeton have?

Name:

Work Space:

Answer:

_____ fire stations

Daily Word Problems

Tuesday-Week 20

Fire Stations

Each fire hose at the La Salle Fire Station is 25 yards long. The station needs enough fire hoses to reach from any fire hydrant to the farthest house, which could be up to 230 feet away. What is the minimum number of hoses that the La Salle Fire Station should have?

Name:

Work Space:

Answer:

_____ hoses

Daily Word Problems
Wednesday-Week 20

Fire Stations

In a recent timed drill, at the sound of the fire alarm it took a fire fighter 9.5 seconds to reach the fire pole, 3.2 seconds to slide down the pole, 13.6 seconds to pull on the protective gear, and 5.7 seconds to climb aboard the fire truck. How long did it take the fire fighter to be ready and aboard the fire truck?

Name:

Work Space:

Answer:

_____ seconds

Daily Word Problems
Thursday-Week 20

Fire Stations

There are 132 fire stations in Miwok. There are 742,236 homes in this huge city. If the fire stations are responsible for an equal number of homes, how many homes is each fire station responsible for?

Name:

Work Space:

Answer:

_____ homes

Daily Word Problems

Friday-Week 20

Fire Stations

N
W ← → E
S

The grid below represents the map of a town. Each rectangle represents a city block. The **Rs** represent blocks of residential homes. There are four fire stations that use a whole block. The **#1** represents Fire Station #1. Use the clues below to determine the locations of the other three fire stations. (Hint: Use three markers to represent each fire station and move them around the grid.)

	R		R		R	R		R	
		R	R			R			R
R		#1	R				R		R
R		R			R				R
R	R								R
R		R		R			R		R
	R							R	
R	R		R	R		R	R	R	R

Clues:

1. The entrance to each fire station is on the northeast corner of the block.

2. No fire stations are located on the perimeter of the city.

3. A truck from Fire Station #1 can drive 4 blocks south and arrive at Fire Station #4's entrance.

4. A truck from Fire Station #2 can drive 6 blocks west and arrive at another fire station's entrance.

5. A truck from Fire Station #3 can drive 3 blocks north and then 2 blocks east and arrive at another fire station's entrance.

Daily Word Problems

Monday—Week 21

Roller-Skating Party

Lincoln Valley Elementary held its annual skating party and $\frac{3}{4}$ of the 400 students came. Of the students who came, $\frac{1}{5}$ brought skates from home. How many students rented skates?

Name:

Work Space:

Answer:

_____ students rented

Daily Word Problems

Tuesday—Week 21

Roller-Skating Party

The roller-skating rink has a perimeter of 150 yards. If the length is twice as long as the width, what are the dimensions of the rink?

Name:

Work Space:

Answer:

_____

Daily Word Problems

Wednesday-Week 21

Roller-Skating Party

Sheila's skates weigh 4 lbs. 3 oz., Heidi's skates weigh 3 lbs. 7 oz., Kieva's skates weigh 5 lbs. 1 oz., and Javier's skates weigh 3 lbs. 13 oz. What is the average weight of the four pairs of skates?

Name:

Work Space:

Answer:

_____

Daily Word Problems

Thursday-Week 21

Roller-Skating Party

Terrell brought $5.00 to spend at the rink's concession stand. Hot dogs cost $0.65, French fries cost $0.80, nachos cost $1.25, and drinks cost $0.95. If Terrell buys French fries and a drink, what is the maximum number of hot dogs he can purchase?

Name:

Work Space:

Answer:

_____ hot dogs

Daily Word Problems

Friday-Week 21

Name:

Roller-Skating Party

Number of Students at the Skating Rink

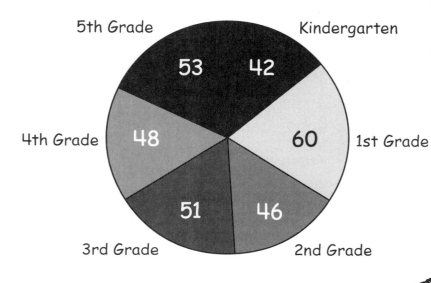

Use the circle graph above to answer the following questions.

• How many third-graders were at the rink? _____

• Were there more second-graders or fourth-graders? _____

• Which grade had the greatest number of students? _____

• Which grade had the fewest number of students? _____

• If you combined fifth grade with second grade and fourth grade with third grade, compare the size of the two groups. _____

Daily Word Problems

Monday—Week 22

Household Chores

Timothy has to take out the trash every day at his house. There are 11 trash cans in his house and it takes him 14 seconds per trash can to empty them into the big trash can in the garage. About how many minutes does he spend emptying the trash in a seven-day week?

Name:

Work Space:

Answer:

_____ minutes

Daily Word Problems

Tuesday—Week 22

Household Chores

Juan bet his mom that he could clean his entire room in less than $7\frac{1}{2}$ minutes. He won his bet with 49 seconds to spare. How long did it take him to clean his room?

Name:

Work Space:

Answer:

_____

Daily Word Problems

Wednesday-Week 22

Household Chores

Name:

Work Space:

Scott has different chores depending on the season. During the 5 warm months, he mows the yard, which takes about $1\frac{1}{2}$ hours each week. During the 7 cold months, he shovels the snow when needed. This winter he shoveled snow for a total of 6 hours. How many hours of chores did he average per month? (Hint: There are 4 weeks in a month.)

Answer:

_____ hours

Daily Word Problems

Thursday-Week 22

Household Chores

Name:

Work Space:

Each week Susie washes dishes three nights, washes clothes one night, empties trash cans two nights, and cooks supper one night. If her Aunt Nancy stopped by randomly one night, what are the chances that Susie would be cooking dinner that night?

Answer:

_____

Daily Word Problems

Friday-Week 22

Household Chores

Each person in the Hunt family washes the dishes on a different night of the week. There are three children (David, Matt, and Shirley) who each wash the dishes one night, while Mom and Dad each wash the dishes two nights during the week. Use the clues below to determine who washes the dishes each night of the week.

When you know that a person and day do **not** go with each other, make an **X** under the day and across from the name. When you know that a name and day do go together, write **YES** in that box. Remember, there will be 2 boxes marked **YES** for both Mom and Dad.

	Sun	Mon	Tues	Wed	Thurs	Fri	Sat
David							
Matt							
Shirley							
Mom							
Dad							

Clues:

1. The week's schedule of chores starts on Sunday and goes through Saturday.

2. Mom's nights are not consecutive nor are Dad's.

3. None of the kids wash the dishes on the weekends.

4. Mom washes the dishes on Monday.

5. David washes dishes on Tuesday and Matt on Thursday OR Matt washes dishes on Tuesday and David on Thursday.

6. Dad washes dishes both of his nights before Shirley and David have their turns.

Daily Word Problems

Monday-Week 23

Computers

Kiko bought a new computer. The tower cost $1,200. The printer cost $269. The monitor cost $159. The speakers cost $129. The scanner cost $219. Kiko also had to pay $35 for shipping and handling to have the computer sent to her home address. What was her total bill without tax?

Name:

Work Space:

Answer:

$ _____

Daily Word Problems

Tuesday-Week 23

Computers

Four elementary schools in the town of Peckham have computers in their classrooms. Centennial has three times as many as Johnson. Johnson has 30 fewer than Jackson. Jackson has 20 more than Clinton. If Clinton has 30 computers, how many computers do the other schools have?

Name:

Work Space:

Answer:

_____ computers at Centennial

_____ computers at Johnson

_____ computers at Jackson

Daily Word Problems

Wednesday-Week 23

Computers

Juanita just got a new monitor for her computer. The rectangular screen is 12 inches tall and 16 inches across. What is the diagonal measurement of the screen? (Hint: Draw a model of the screen using centimeters.)

Name:

Work Space:

Answer:

_____ inches

Daily Word Problems

Thursday-Week 23

Computers

There are three children in the Shelley family, and they have been saving their summer money to purchase a new computer. To be able to afford the new computer, they are going to split the cost among the three of them. If the entire system costs $2,172, how much will each person have to contribute?

Name:

Work Space:

Answer:

$_____

Name:

Computers

Jesse has saved money in several places to buy a new computer. He has $750 in his savings account, $300 in his bank at home, and a gift card for $500. He saw this advertisement for a laptop.

COMPUTERS 4 LESS

Gaming laptop with 17″ display, normally $1,720

SALE this week only! 25% off!

• Does Jesse have enough money to buy the computer? Why or why not? (Hint: Remember that 25% is the same as $\frac{1}{4}$.)

_____

_____

_____

_____

Daily Word Problems

Monday-Week 24

Spelling Bee

The director of the regional spelling bee wants to charge a small fee to cover the contest costs. The total cost to put on the event is about $195. If there are going to be approximately 65 participants, how much should each person be charged to cover the costs of the day?

Name:

Work Space:

Answer:

$ _____

Daily Word Problems

Tuesday-Week 24

Spelling Bee

At the beginning of the spelling bee there were 60 participants. One-third of the participants were eliminated during the first round. One-fourth of the remaining participants were eliminated during the second round. One-sixth of the remaining participants were eliminated during the third round. How many participants were still competing at the beginning of the fourth round?

Name:

Work Space:

Answer:

_____ participants

Daily Word Problems

Wednesday-Week 24

Spelling Bee

Jamie won the spelling bee. She completed 8 more rounds than Antonio, who completed three times as many rounds as Beth. If Beth completed 6 rounds, how many rounds did Jamie complete?

Name:

Work Space:

Answer:

_____ rounds

Daily Word Problems

Thursday-Week 24

Spelling Bee

Three of the words in the spelling bee were *decagon, hexagon,* and *octagon.* Someone noticed that all three of these words end with the suffix *gon.* What do you think is the meaning of this suffix?

Name:

Work Space:

Answer:

_____

_____

_____

_____

Daily Word Problems

Friday-Week 24

Spelling Bee

Use the following clues to figure out the schedule for the day of the spelling bee.

Clues:

1. There were 13 hours between the time registration opened and the time the awards ceremony was completed.

2. There were two 15-minute breaks that began five hours apart from each other.

3. The spelling bee started $1\frac{1}{2}$ hours after registration started.

4. The $1\frac{1}{2}$-hour lunch break started at noon, which was two hours after the morning break.

5. The awards ceremony lasted $1\frac{1}{2}$ hours.

6. The afternoon break started $3\frac{1}{2}$ hours before the awards ceremony began.

7. The spelling bee contest was finished $8\frac{1}{2}$ hours after the event started.

_____   _____
_____   _____
_____   _____
_____   _____
_____   _____
_____   _____
_____   _____

Daily Word Problems

Monday-Week 25

Ice-Cream Parlor

Ted's dad agreed to take out the eight players on Ted's basketball team for ice-cream sundaes. Each of the players ordered an ice-cream sundae for $2.49. What was the total bill?

Name:

Work Space:

Answer:

$_____

Daily Word Problems

Tuesday-Week 25

Ice-Cream Parlor

One scoop of ice cream weighs about 3 ounces. Last Thursday the ice-cream parlor used 18 pounds of ice cream. About how many scoops of ice cream were served last Thursday?

Name:

Work Space:

Answer:

_____ scoops

Daily Word Problems • EMC 3005

Daily Word Problems

Wednesday-Week 25

Ice-Cream Parlor

The most popular treat at the ice-cream parlor is the double-scoop cone. If a chocolate scoop on top of a strawberry scoop is the same cone as strawberry on top of chocolate, how many different double-scoop cones can be made with six flavors of ice cream? (Remember, someone could have two scoops of one flavor of ice cream.)

Name:

Work Space:

Answer:

_____ combinations

Daily Word Problems

Thursday-Week 25

Ice-Cream Parlor

Doris's bill at the ice-cream parlor comes to $2.54. She realizes that she doesn't have any dollar bills, so she is paying with coins. She has 24 coins including quarters, dimes, nickels, and pennies. She has the same number of nickels as quarters and twice as many dimes as quarters. If she has 5 nickels, how many quarters, dimes, and pennies does she have?

Name:

Work Space:

Answer:

_____ quarters

_____ dimes

_____ pennies

Name:

Ice-Cream Parlor

The ice-cream parlor has the following floor plan.

50 feet

10 feet

30 feet

12 feet

• What is the area of the store? _____

Daily Word Problems

Monday-Week 26

Clothing Sale

Sixteen blouses are on sale at Debbie's Boutique. Each blouse was originally priced at $36.00. The sale price of each blouse is only $24.50. How much would all the blouses cost?

Name:

Work Space:

Answer:

$_____

Daily Word Problems

Tuesday-Week 26

Clothing Sale

Marx's clothing store is selling a lot of items. On Monday 495 items were sold. On Tuesday 450 items were sold. On Friday 593 items were sold. Marx's misplaced the totals for Wednesday and Thursday, but the average over the five days was 494 items per day. What could have been the totals for Wednesday and Thursday?

Name:

Work Space:

Answer:

_____ items on Wednesday

_____ items on Thursday

Daily Word Problems
Wednesday-Week 26

Clothing Sale

Raymond and his three sisters want to buy a new outfit for their mom for her birthday. The total bill is $132. If they split the cost equally, how much does each person need to contribute?

Name:

Work Space:

Answer:

$_____

Daily Word Problems
Thursday-Week 26

Clothing Sale

Pete wants to buy a stack of clothing that totals $200. The sales tax is 6%. If you add the tax to his total bill, what is Pete's grand total?

Name:

Work Space:

Answer:

$_____

Daily Word Problems

Name:

Clothing Sale

Use the following graph to answer the questions below.

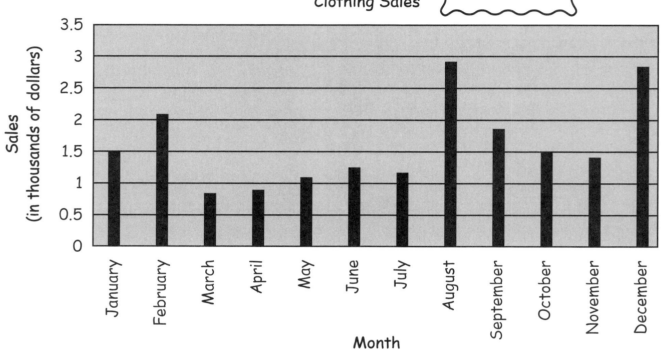

Clothing Sales

* About how much more was sold in August than in July?

_____

* What is the range of the months' sales?

_____

* Give one reason why August might have been one of the highest selling months for clothing.

_____

_____

_____

_____

Daily Word Problems

Monday-Week 27

Rodeo

The rodeo started 7 minutes late. It was scheduled to last 3 hours, but it ran 22 minutes longer. If the rodeo ended at 9:59 p.m., at what time did it begin?

Name:

Work Space:

Answer:

_____

Daily Word Problems

Tuesday-Week 27

Rodeo

On Friday night 2,950 people attended the rodeo, and 3,159 people attended on Saturday night. If the stadium seats 4,000 people, how many empty seats were there for the two nights?

Name:

Work Space:

Answer:

_____ seats

Daily Word Problems

Wednesday-Week 27

Rodeo

Tickets to the rodeo sell for $12 each. If they are bought in groups of 10 or more, you receive $\frac{1}{4}$ off the price of each ticket. Julie wants to buy 14 tickets. How much will her total cost be for the 14 tickets?

Name:

Work Space:

Answer:

$ _____

Daily Word Problems

Thursday-Week 27

Rodeo

The arena where the rodeo takes place is an oval shape with a perimeter of 225 yards. The fencing that is planned for around the arena is sold by the foot. How many feet of fencing are needed?

Name:

Work Space:

Answer:

_____ feet

Name:

Rodeo

In the Bucking Bronco competition, ribbons were awarded to the top five winners. Use the clues below to determine the place (highest rank is 1st) that each of the five people finished.

When you know that a name and rank do **not** go with each other, make an X under the rank and across from the name. When you know that a name and rank do go together, write YES in that box. You can then X that name and rank for all others.

	1st	2nd	3rd	4th	5th
Kevin					
Michael					
Dean					
John					
Drew					

Clues:

1. The sum of Kevin and Michael's places equals the place of Dean.

2. John's place was one rank lower than Drew's.

3. Michael's rank was one higher than Dean's.

4. Dean did not place third.

Daily Word Problems

Monday-Week 28

School Cafeteria

Lunch at Samantha's school costs $1.15 per day. She brought a $10.00 bill and wants to pay for five lunches for that week. How much change should she receive?

Name:

Work Space:

Answer:

$ _____

Daily Word Problems

Tuesday-Week 28

School Cafeteria

The school cafeteria offers three choices for the main course (peanut butter and jelly sandwich, burrito, or fish sticks) and two choices for the side dish (vegetables or potatoes) and three choices for the dessert (ice cream, brownie, or cookies). How many different combinations can the students order from these choices?

Name:

Work Space:

Answer:

_____ combinations

Daily Word Problems

Wednesday-Week 28

School Cafeteria

Yesterday the cafeteria collected $91.35 for milk. If each milk cost $0.35, how many milks were purchased yesterday?

Name:

Work Space:

Answer:

_____ milks

Daily Word Problems

Thursday-Week 28

School Cafeteria

The adult meals in the school cafeteria cost $2.35. Mrs. Rockwell would like to purchase seven lunches in advance. What amount should she write on her check?

Name:

Work Space:

Answer:

$_____

Name:

The following list shows the proportions of cookies that are served in the cafeteria. If there are 544 cookies served, how many of each type are served?

$\frac{1}{4}$ peanut butter cookies

$\frac{1}{8}$ snickerdoodle cookies

$\frac{1}{4}$ chocolate chip cookies

$\frac{1}{8}$ oatmeal raisin cookies

$\frac{1}{4}$ sugar cookies

_____

_____

_____

_____

_____

Daily Word Problems

Monday-Week 29

Doctor's Appointments

The rectangular-shaped doctor's office has an area of 120 square feet and a perimeter of 44 feet. What are the dimensions of this office space?

Name:

Work Space:

Answer:

_____

Daily Word Problems

Tuesday-Week 29

Doctor's Appointments

Toby went in for his annual physical and found out that he had doubled his weight from two years ago when he weighed a third of his mom's weight. Since then, his mom has gained 26 pounds and now weighs 149 pounds. How much does Toby currently weigh?

Name:

Work Space:

Answer:

_____ pounds

Daily Word Problems

Wednesday-Week 29

Doctor's Appointments

Mark's doctor's appointment was 35 minutes after Tyson's appointment. Tyson's appointment was 20 minutes after Timothy's appointment. Timothy arrived 8 minutes before his appointment, but 17 minutes after Raul's appointment, which started at 9:30 a.m. At what time did Mark's appointment start?

Name:

Work Space:

Answer:

_____

Daily Word Problems

Thursday-Week 29

Doctor's Appointments

Marissa had a doctor's appointment last Friday. The bill for her visit came to $345. Her family's health insurance will pay 80% of the bill. What is the dollar figure that Marissa's family will have to pay? (Hint: Remember that 80% is the same as $\frac{4}{5}$.)

Name:

Work Space:

Answer:

$_____

Name:

Doctor's Appointments

Using the following graph, what can you say about Victor's growth compared to the average growth for males?

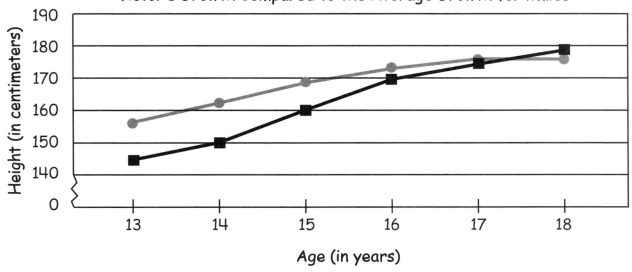

Victor's Growth Compared to the Average Growth for Males

_____

_____

_____

_____

_____

Daily Word Problems

Monday-Week 30

Library

There are four shelves of books along a wall in the library. On the top shelf, 16 of the 126 books are checked out. On the second shelf, 8 of the 137 books are checked out. On the third shelf, 29 of the 119 books are checked out. On the bottom shelf, 17 of the 138 books are checked out. How many books are currently on the four shelves?

Name:

Work Space:

Answer:

_____ books

Daily Word Problems

Tuesday-Week 30

Library

The librarian was checking the thicknesses of several books and found that the average thickness of a book was 1.8 centimeters. She found this by averaging the thicknesses of five different books. Four of the thicknesses were 1.4 cm, 1.9 cm, 2.1 cm, and 2.4 cm. What was the thickness of the fifth book that she measured?

Name:

Work Space:

Answer:

_____ cm

Daily Word Problems
Wednesday-Week 30

Library

The library is purchasing new library books. They have chosen 29 books that each sell for $3.95. How much will all the books cost?

Name:

Work Space:

Answer:

$_____

Daily Word Problems
Thursday-Week 30

Library

The first shelf of one bookcase is 2 in. off the ground. The second shelf is 1 ft. 5 in. above the first. The third shelf is 1 ft. 3 in. above the second. The fourth shelf is 1 ft. 2 in. above the third. The top shelf is 1 ft. 4 in. above the fourth. How high off the ground is the top shelf?

Name:

Work Space:

Answer:

_____

Name:

There are tables with tops shaped like a trapezoid all around the library. The librarian grouped 3 tables to form a triangle and 16 tables to form a parallelogram. Show what these arrangements look like, using the trapezoids below.

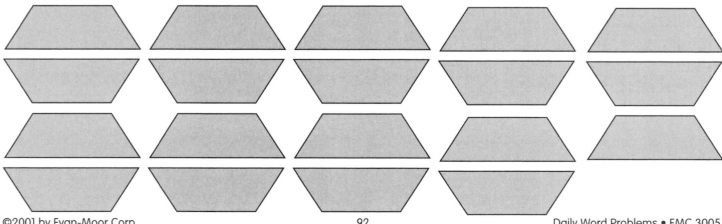

Daily Word Problems
Monday-Week 31

Pizza

Stephanie's family went out for pizza. They ordered a large pizza for $16.99, a pitcher of soda for $2.25, and three side salads for $1.19 each. If they paid for lunch with two twenty-dollar bills, what change did they receive? (This restaurant includes the tax in its prices.)

Name:

Work Space:

Answer:

$ _____

Daily Word Problems
Tuesday-Week 31

Pizza

Jimmy and four of his friends are going out for pizza. They ordered two large pizzas that are each divided into eight slices. How many pieces does each person get?

Name:

Work Space:

Answer:

_____ slices

Daily Word Problems

Wednesday-Week 31

Pizza

At the Grand Pizza Parlor there are six different meat toppings for the pizzas: Italian sausage, hamburger, pepperoni, ham, bacon, and pork sausage. There are also three different kinds of cheeses: mozzarella, parmesan, and American cheese. If the standard pizza comes with two different meat toppings and one cheese topping, how many different combinations of pizzas are possible?

Name:

Work Space:

Answer:

_____ combinations

Daily Word Problems

Thursday-Week 31

Pizza

Mr. Call's class is ordering pizzas to have a pizza party. They decide to order 7 large pizzas that are each priced at $8.95. How much will all the pizzas cost without tax?

Name:

Work Space:

Answer:

$_____

Name:

Pizza

The entire fifth grade at Ruben Elementary School decided to order pizza. Use the clues below to determine what is on each of the 16 pizzas.

Clues:

1. One-fourth of the pizzas have just cheese.

2. One-third of the remaining pizzas have pepperoni only.

3. One-fourth of the remaining pizzas have mushrooms and sausage.

4. Half of the remaining pizzas have ham and pineapple.

5. One-third of the remaining pizzas have black olives and mushrooms.

6. Half of the remaining pizzas have hamburger.

7. Half of the final pizza has anchovies and mushrooms, while the other half has green peppers and bacon.

_____

_____

_____

_____

_____

_____

_____

Daily Word Problems

Monday-Week 32

Miniature Golf

Max and his friends played miniature golf at the new *Goofy Golf*. Max completed the west section in 35 minutes and the east section in 41 minutes. Jordan finished the west section in 37 minutes and the east section in 42 minutes. Gerardo finished the west section in 29 minutes and the east section in 45 minutes. Who finished both sections in the fastest time?

Name:

Work Space:

Answer:

_____

Daily Word Problems

Tuesday-Week 32

Miniature Golf

Susie got the following scores for the first 18 holes of miniature golf: 3, 4, 2, 1, 4, 4, 2, 3, 4, 3, 2, 1, 2, 3, 3, 5, 4, and 3. If par for the first 18 holes is 45 strokes, is Susie's stroke total over, under, or equal to par?

Name:

Work Space:

Answer:

_____

Daily Word Problems

Wednesday-Week 32

Miniature Golf

Sammy loves miniature golf. Last year he played 572 games of miniature golf. Assuming that Sammy played the same number of games each week, how many games per week did Sammy play last year? (Hint: There are 52 weeks in a year.)

Name:

Work Space:

Answer:

_____ games per week

Daily Word Problems

Thursday-Week 32

Miniature Golf

The distance from the starting point to the hole on the first green is 108 inches. The distance on the second green to the hole is 4 yards. On the third green, the distance to the hole is 13 feet. Which of the first three greens has the longest distance to the hole?

Name:

Work Space:

Answer:

_____

Daily Word Problems

Name:

Miniature Golf

The outdoor carpeting on the 18th green has become worn and needs to be replaced. The cost of the carpeting is $2.57 per square foot. Using the diagram below, figure out how many square feet of carpet will be needed and what the total cost will be.

8 feet

2 feet

6 feet

6 feet

4 feet

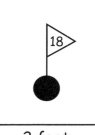
18

2 feet

_____

_____

Daily Word Problems

Monday-Week 33

Garden Planting

Sunnyside Elementary is considering starting a school garden. If each class wants to tend twelve square feet of garden and there are 27 classes, what would be the total size of the garden?

Name:

Work Space:

Answer:

_____ square feet

Daily Word Problems

Tuesday-Week 33

Garden Planting

Mr. Kincaid's class wants to plant $\frac{1}{4}$ of its 12-foot-square plot with tomatoes. Of the remaining garden, $\frac{1}{3}$ will be peas. Of the rest of the plot, $\frac{1}{2}$ will be radishes and $\frac{1}{2}$ will be lettuce. How many square feet of radishes will the class plant?

Name:

Work Space:

Answer:

_____ square feet

Daily Word Problems

Wednesday-Week 33

Garden Planting

One area of the school garden is a rectangular-shaped plot that is 13 feet long. If the fence that surrounds the garden is 38 feet long, what is the width of the garden?

Name:

Work Space:

Answer:

_____ feet

Daily Word Problems

Thursday-Week 33

Garden Planting

Mrs. Ramirez's class was getting ready to plant tomatoes. They were wondering if each package of tomato seeds contained the same number of seeds. They counted the seeds in four packages and found that there was an average of 73 seeds in the packages. The first three packages contained 78, 71, and 74 seeds, respectively. How many seeds were in the fourth package?

Name:

Work Space:

Answer:

_____ seeds

Daily Word Problems

Friday-Week 33

Name:

Garden Planting

Use the following graph to answer the questions below.

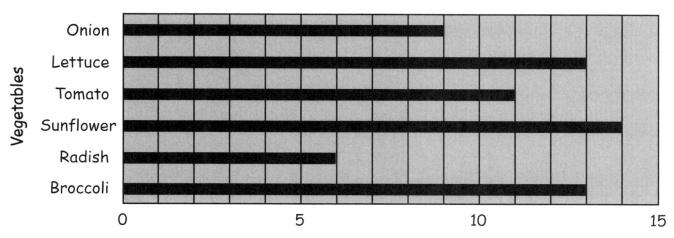

Days from Planting to Sprouting

(Vegetables: Onion, Lettuce, Tomato, Sunflower, Radish, Broccoli — Number of Days: 0, 5, 10, 15)

• How many days were there between when
the first vegetables sprouted and when the
last vegetables sprouted? _____

• What was the last plant to sprout? _____

• What was the average number of days it
took for the plants to sprout? _____

Daily Word Problems

Monday-Week 34

Newspaper Delivery

Jennifer delivers newspapers and she figures that she makes about 7¢ per newspaper each day of delivery. If she delivers 48 newspapers each day, how much does she make during one 7-day week?

Name:

Work Space:

Answer:

$ _____

Daily Word Problems

Tuesday-Week 34

Newspaper Delivery

Juan delivers papers every morning before he goes to school. He has to have all the papers delivered by 6:30 a.m. He has 86 papers and he figures it takes him an average of $1\frac{1}{2}$ minutes to deliver each paper. At what time must he start in order to be done as close to 6:30 as possible?

Name:

Work Space:

Answer:

_____

Daily Word Problems

Wednesday-Week 34

Newspaper Delivery

The Dirk family tips their newspaper carrier for delivering the newspaper. They tip 10% of what they pay for the subscription. They paid $20 in tips for the entire year. How much does their newspaper subscription cost a year?

Name:

Work Space:

Answer:

$_____

Daily Word Problems

Thursday-Week 34

Newspaper Delivery

Neil found out that the Sunday paper that he delivers weighs about 1 pound 12 ounces. He delivers 39 newspapers on Sundays. How much do the 39 newspapers weigh? (Hint: 16 ounces = 1 pound)

Name:

Work Space:

Answer:

_____

Newspaper Delivery

Use the clues below to determine the number of newspapers that each carrier delivers.

As you read the clues, fill in the number of **newspapers** in the top row. When you know that a name and number of newspapers do **not** go with each other, make an **X** under the number of newspapers and across from the name. When you know that a name and number of newspapers do go together, write **YES** in that box. You can then **X** that name and number of newspapers for all others.

Angela						
Cathy						
Christine						
Alec						
Austin						
Barry						
Ben						

Clues:

1. The fewest newspapers anyone delivers is 32.

2. Three kids deliver numbers of newspapers in the 30s, two kids in the 40s, one kid in the 50s, and one kid in the 60s.

3. One of the girls delivers 38 newspapers.

4. Cathy delivers the most newspapers, which is 20 more than Barry.

5. The number of newspapers for the three kids who have names that start with A are in the 30s.

6. Christine delivers 1 more newspaper than Alec, who delivers 39 papers.

7. Barry delivers 10 more newspapers than Austin.

8. Ben delivers 11 more than Christine.

Daily Word Problems

Monday-Week 35

Summer Camps

Harry is going to a summer camp that will cost $620. He has not yet saved any money. If he has only 8 weeks to earn the money, how much does he need to earn each week to attend the camp?

Name:

Work Space:

Answer:

$_____

Daily Word Problems

Tuesday-Week 35

Summer Camps

Gretchen needs to send in her camp registration form. The postage needed to mail in her oversized letter is 96¢. She looked in her pocket and saw that she has 14 coins that add up to 96¢. She has the same number of quarters as nickels and the same number of dimes as pennies. What coins does she have?

Name:

Work Space:

Answer:

_____ quarter(s)

_____ dime(s)

_____ nickel(s)

_____ penny(ies)

Daily Word Problems

Wednesday-Week 35

Summer Camps

Tim and Jorge hope they will be assigned to the same cabin at summer camp. Each cabin has 8 beds in it, and Tim knows that he is staying in the green cabin and not the red cabin. If there are 14 boys going to camp in addition to Tim and Jorge, what is the chance that Tim and Jorge will both be in the green cabin?

Name:

Work Space:

Answer:

_____

Daily Word Problems

Thursday-Week 35

Summer Camps

Cole's sleeping bag has four sides. The side with the zipper is parallel to the opposite side. None of the angles where the sides meet are right angles. The side opposite the zipper is shorter than the side with the zipper. The other two sides are the same length. What shape is Cole's sleeping bag?

Name:

Work Space:

Answer:

_____

Name:

Summer Camps

Camp Watchoo is located on a large piece of land with a sizable amount of acreage. Use the following figure (representing the piece of land) to determine the amount of acreage. Round your answer to the nearest acre. (Hint: An acre is equal to 4,840 square yards.)

583 yards

300 yards

300 yards

950 yards

Daily Word Problems

Monday-Week 36

Summer Spending Money

During the last five months, Nancy has been saving money for the summer. During January she saved $22. During February she saved $36. During March she saved $29. During April she saved $18, after buying her sister a $12 birthday present. During May she saved $27. How much has she saved in all?

Name:

Work Space:

Answer:

$_____

Daily Word Problems

Tuesday-Week 36

Summer Spending Money

Over the last year, Stormy and her two sisters saved money for their family trip this summer. They are now getting ready for the trip and want to know how much they can spend on each of the 15 days of their trip. If they saved a total of $420, what is the total amount all three girls can spend each day?

Name:

Work Space:

Answer:

$_____

Daily Word Problems

Wednesday-Week 36

Summer Spending Money

Josie is earning money by painting her fence. Her parents will pay her 25¢ for every linear foot she paints. The fence is 15 yards down one side and 18 yards across the back. The fences on the other two sides have already been painted. How much money will Josie earn?

Name:

Work Space:

Answer:

$ _____

Daily Word Problems

Thursday-Week 36

Summer Spending Money

Ian has been saving money for his summer trip to his grandparents' house. He has saved 18 bills of varying denominations, including twenties, tens, fives, and ones. He's saved a total of $126. He has the same number of tens as he has ones. How many of each bill does Ian have?

Name:

Work Space:

Answer:

_____ twenties

_____ tens

_____ fives

_____ ones

Daily Word Problems

Name: _____

Summer Spending Money

Use the clues below to determine how much money each person has saved for his or her trip and where each person is going this summer.

When you know that a name and amount of money OR a name and state do **not** go with each other, make an **X** under the money or state and across from the name. When you know that a name and amount of money or a name and state do go together, write **YES** in that box. You can then **X** that name and money or name and state for all others.

	$25	$48	$72	$95	$120	$210	AZ	CA	CO	FL	ND	NY
Katie												
Lauren												
Holly												
Dave												
Brett												
Jon												

Clues:

1. If you add the money that Katie and Lauren have saved together, you get $120.

2. If you add the money that Holly and Dave have saved together, you get $120.

3. Brett has saved more money than Jon.

4. The person who saved $120 is going to Arizona.

5. Holly is going to one of the states whose name begins with the letter N.

6. Brett is going to Tampa on his trip.

7. Neither Lauren nor Dave is going to North Dakota.

8. The person going to New York has more money than the person going to California or North Dakota, but less money than the person going to Colorado.

9. Dave has $48 saved.

10. Lauren is going to Colorado this summer for her trip.

         Daily Word Problems • EMC 3005

Answer Key

Week 1
Monday—10 for $1 is the better buy because you would only get 8 tickets for four quarters.
Tuesday—8 people
Wednesday—about 486 students
Thursday—Kindergarten-$400, 1st-$800, 2nd-$200, 3rd-$800, 4th-$400, 5th-$200
Friday—Penny, because you can't have more than fifty points. Ian, because you can't get an odd sum when you add up only even numbers.

Week 2
Monday—784 feet
Tuesday—2,500 Caramels
Wednesday—216 Almond Bars
Thursday—7:12 a.m.
Friday—February and December; Holidays like Valentines Day, Christmas or Hanukkah; $60,000 more in February

Week 3
Monday—375 square feet
Tuesday—21 pounds
Wednesday—31 baskets
Thursday—10 combinations
Friday—371 total items; 3 pounds per watermelon; 0.2 OR 1/5 pound per pepper

Week 4
Monday—372,450 points
Tuesday—15 combinations
Wednesday—3,375 points
Thursday—$8.50
Friday—Started at I, Friend's house was at D

Week 5
Monday—17 cabins in all—8 for boys, 9 for girls
Tuesday—$3,650.00
Wednesday—Jorge's sleeping bag
Thursday—

Boys' Cabin   Girls' Cabin

Friday—The boys' names are George Moore, Mike Bucklen, Raul McClain, Sam Brown, Saul Mitchell, and Tim Sari.

Week 6
Monday—$5.20
Tuesday—4 dogs
Wednesday—$75
Thursday—3,600 feet
Friday—19 total dogs; 3 answers are possible:
poodles (8) = German Shepherds (5) + Black Labs (3);
German Shepherds (5) = Black Labs (3) + Irish Setters (2);
Black Labs (3) = Irish Setters (2) + Saint Bernards (1)

Week 7
Monday—one-half hour OR 30 minutes
Tuesday—20 books
Wednesday—10.1 cm
Thursday—15 hours per student
Friday—Timm's class read the most with 92 books; Timm's average was 30 2/3 books per week, Kehl's average was 23 books per week, and Bennett's average was 25 1/3 books per week

Week 8
Monday—Jim-50 minutes, Suzanne-20 minutes
Tuesday—2,112 keys
Wednesday—Possible dimensions: 5 x 3, 6 x 2, and 7 x 1
Thursday—8/52 OR 2/13
Friday—$7.00

Week 9
Monday—45 fish
Tuesday—Beth-5 hamsters, Kristen-3 birds, Wendi-2 dogs, John-2 cats
Wednesday—20 pounds and 40 pounds
Thursday—1 sheet of plywood
Friday—A=3 feet, B=4 feet, C=5 feet, D=6 feet, E=8 feet, F=10 feet

Week 10
Monday—Jimmy & Joe-72 laps, Sally-78 laps
Tuesday—125 miles
Wednesday—5.6 seconds
Thursday—24 gallons
Friday—The names are Angel Turnwall, Austin Tjardes, Ben Jones, George Brown, and Sarah Chavez.

Week 11
Monday—4 computer stores
Tuesday—$17.47
Wednesday—7 quarters, 3 dimes, 2 nickels
Thursday—128 feet 4 inches
Friday—Store B has the larger area, with 608 square feet compared to 396 square feet.

Week 12
Monday—Total of 110 minutes (Mrs. Johnson-50 minutes, Mr. Beach-25 minutes, Mrs. Rodriquez-35 minutes)
Tuesday—reading
Wednesday—8,100 minutes
Thursday—Total=880 minutes, difference=145 minutes
Friday—Answers may vary, but should be close to the following: math-45 minutes, reading-60 minutes, science-25 minutes, history-35 minutes, spelling-35 minutes.

Week 13
Monday—6,572 pounds
Tuesday—$14.58
Wednesday—Answers will vary, but should be close to 7,408 pounds.
Thursday—3,774 tubes
Friday—Room 2-10 pounds, Room 4-18 pounds, Room 6-23 pounds, Room 7-15 pounds, Room 9-12 pounds, Room 10-7 pounds

Week 14
Monday—20 loads
Tuesday—Soap-$4.98, Fabric Softener-$2.49
Wednesday—38 feet 8 inches
Thursday—5 socks because the first four socks could each be a different color. The fifth sock would match one of the first four.
Friday—32.2 minutes

Week 15
Monday—$21.80
Tuesday—2:35 p.m.
Wednesday—220 feet
Thursday—1,188 people
Friday—52 triangles

Week 16
Monday—$1,842.50
Tuesday—1,132 people
Wednesday—61.3 degrees
Thursday—42 rides
Friday—range of adults-90, total number of children-1,550

Week 17
Monday—2 hours 55 minutes
Tuesday—124 flights
Wednesday—12 ways—A=Abe, B=Ben, M=Mom, D=Dad—ABMD, ABDM, MABD, DABM, MDAB, DMAB, BAMD, BADM, MBAD, DBAM, MDBA, DMBA
Thursday—Yes, they can all ride in the elevator because they weigh only 770 lbs. in all.
Friday—Stang-#1726, Fortner-#1536, Christopher-#2608, Fitch-#1834, Smythe-#1428

Week 18
Monday—39 people
Tuesday—15 hours
Wednesday—9:35 a.m.
Thursday—$12.56
Friday—Range-75, Median-60

Week 19
Monday—$840,000
Tuesday—

Wednesday—$7,500 per month
Thursday—2 minutes left
Friday—$5,750

Week 20
Monday—12 stations
Tuesday—4 hoses
Wednesday—32 seconds
Thursday—5,623 homes
Friday—

	R		R		R	R		R	
		R	R				R			R
R		#1	R				R	#2	R
R		R			R				R
R	R								R
R		R		R		#3	R		R
	R	#4						R	
R	R		R	R		R	R	R	R

Week 21
Monday—240 students
Tuesday—25 yards by 50 yards
Wednesday—4 pounds 2 ounces
Thursday—5 hot dogs
Friday—
   1. 51 third-graders
   2. There were more fourth-graders.
   3. 1st grade
   4. Kindergarten
   5. Both groups would be equal in size.

Week 22
Monday—about 18 minutes
Tuesday—6 minutes 41 seconds
Wednesday—3 hours per month
Thursday—1/7
Friday—David-Thursday, Matt-Tuesday, Shirley-Friday,
   Mom-Monday & Saturday, Dad-Sunday & Wednesday

Week 23
Monday—$2,011
Tuesday—Centennial-60, Johnson-20, Jackson-50
Wednesday—20 inches
Thursday—$724
Friday—Yes, the computer will cost $1,290 and he has
   saved $1,550.

Week 24
Monday—$3/person
Tuesday—25 participants
Wednesday—26 rounds
Thursday—two-dimensional figure with the number of sides
   (and angles) as the prefix (for example, octagon is an
   eight-sided 2-dimensional figure)
Friday—The schedule for the day is:

7:00 a.m.	registration opened
8:30 a.m.	spelling bee contest began
10:00-10:15 a.m.	morning break
12:00-1:30 p.m.	lunch break
3:00-3:15 p.m.	afternoon break
5:00 p.m.	spelling bee completed
6:30 p.m.	awards ceremony started
8:00 p.m.	awards ceremony completed

Week 25
Monday—$19.92
Tuesday—about 96 scoops
Wednesday—21 combinations
Thursday—5 quarters, 10 dimes, and 4 pennies
Friday—740 square feet

Week 26
Monday—$392
Tuesday—Answers will vary, but the sum of Wednesday and
   Thursday should equal 932 items.
Wednesday—$33/person
Thursday—$212
Friday—$1,700; $2,100; Answers will vary. For example:
   Students are starting back to school and they purchase
   a lot of new school clothes.

Week 27
Monday—6:37 p.m.
Tuesday—1,891 empty seats
Wednesday—$126
Thursday—675 feet
Friday—Kevin-1st, Michael-4th, Dean-5th, John-3rd, Drew-2nd

Week 28
Monday—$4.25
Tuesday—18 combinations
Wednesday—261 milks
Thursday—$16.45
Friday—136 peanut butter, 68 snickerdoodle, 136 chocolate chip,
   68 oatmeal raisin, and 136 sugar

Week 29
Monday—10 feet by 12 feet
Tuesday—82 pounds
Wednesday—10:50 a.m.
Thursday—$69
Friday—Answers will vary. For example: Victor's growth spurt
   happened later than the average male OR Victor surpassed
   the average height around 17 years of age.

Week 30
Monday—450 books
Tuesday—1.2 cm
Wednesday—$114.55
Thursday—5 feet 4 inches
Friday—

triangle

parallelogram